Beauceron
20 Milestone Challenges

Beauceron Memorable Moments. Includes Milestones for Memories, Gifts, Socialization & Training

Volume 1

Todays Doggy

Dedicated To All of You Wonderful Owners and Fans

Introduction

Welcome to the Original Doggy Milestone Series™ where you are encouraged to create those special moments with your dog. We have composed the milestones in a way that challenges you to set the stage before taking your photos.

Use props and make it fun - be creative in setting up your photos. Get family and friends involved - take it out with you - use it in different places and settings - have a play with it and most importantly, have a good time!

You can either hold the desired milestone spread open yourself - or have somebody hold it open as you take the snap.

If you would like to have the selected milestone book spread open and standing independently in your photos, you can use one or two large 'foldback' clips to hold the spread open.

Good luck and enjoy your photo fun.

I Love My Family...

...And My Family Loves Me

At The Beach!

Having a Wave of a Time

NIGHT

OUT

With My Doggy Pals

IT'S...

BED TIME

I DIDN'T KNOW WHICH STICK YOU THREW

SO I BOUGHT BACK ALL OF THEM

They Say Diamonds Are a Girl's Best Friend

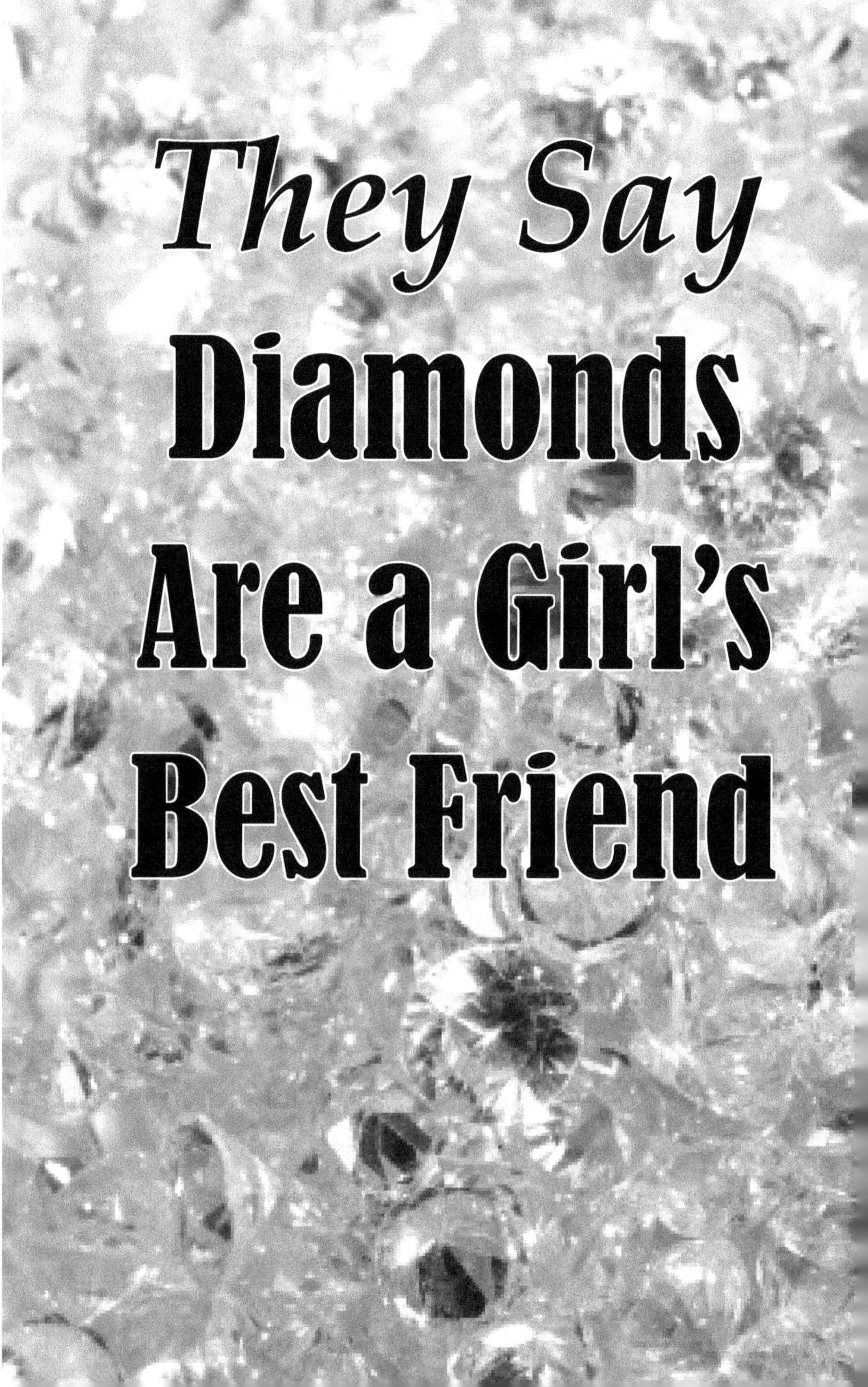

I Disagree! I'm The Only "*Best Friend*" Here!

I'm Going To Start Eating Healthy...

Next Week!

DO
NOT
DISTURB

PLAYING IN THE LEAVES

I Need
a
HUGe

Amount of Treats

Say

ello

To My Little Friend

OFF To The VET??

CATCH ME IF YOU CAN!

KEEP
CALM

WE'RE
A
TEAM

NASA Wants To Hire Me

Because I'm a STAR!

OOPS!
I
Buried
Your
Stuff

...But I Forgot Where

I’m a Super Hero

My Real Name Is SUPER POOCH

VIP

Very Incredible Pup

I DIDN'T DO IT

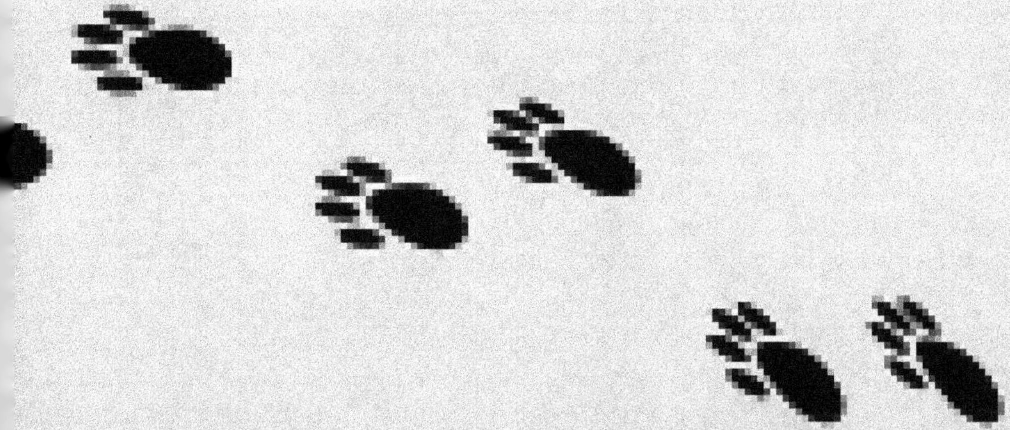

I'll Just Be Over Here...

Looking Fabulous

PLEASE

PLEASE

PRETTY
PLEEEASE

CAN I KEEP IT?

I’m On a SEAFOOD Diet

When I SEE FOOD, I EAT IT!

CPSIA information can be obtained
at www.ICGtesting.com
Printed in the USA
LVHW080544200819
628164LV00008B/566/P

9 781395 321680